Noah's Wife

WRITTEN BY

Marty Rhodes Figley STACKS

ILLUSTRATED BY

Anita Riggio

EERDMANS BOOKS FOR YOUNG READERS   GRAND RAPIDS, MICHIGAN   CAMBRIDGE, U.K.

For my parents, a great pair — M. R. F.
For Olivia and Liza — A. R.

Text copyright © 1998 by Marty Rhodes Figley
Illustrations copyright © 1998 by Anita Riggio

Published 1998 by Eerdmans Books for Young Readers
an imprint of Wm. B. Eerdmans Publishing Co.
255 Jefferson Ave. S.E.,
Grand Rapids, Michigan 49503
PO. Box 163, Cambridge CB3 9PU U.K.

Printed in Hong Kong

02 01 00 99 98   7 6 5 4 3 2 1

LIBRARY OF CONGRESS CATALOGING-IN-PUBLICATION DATA

Figley, Marty Rhodes, 1948-
Noah's wife / by Marty Figley; illustrated by Anita Riggio.
p.   cm.
Summary: A retelling of the Biblical flood story focusing on Noah's wife and how preparations for the flood disrupted her life, but how she accepted these disruptions in trust and faith.
ISBN 0-8028-5107-X (cloth: alk. paper)
ISBN 0-8028-5133-9 (pbk.: alk. paper)
*   1.Noah's ark—juvenile literature. 2. Noah's wife (Biblical figure)—juvenile literature.*
3.Bible stories, English - O.T. Genesis. [I. Noah's ark. 2. Noah's wife (Biblical figure).
3.Bible stories - O.T. I 1. Riggio, Anita, ill. II. Title.
*   BS658.F53 1998*
*   222'.1109505 - dc2O   95-31044*
*   CIP*
*   AC*

The illustrations were done in watercolor and gouache.
The text was set in Usherwood Book.
The book was designed by Joy Chu.

A long time ago there lived a
righteous man named Noah. He
had a very good wife.

She was very good at hugging their three sons, tending the vegetable garden, and running a peaceful house. But Noah's wife would sometimes get exasperated.

And the person who could exasperate her the most was the person she loved the most — Noah.

Noah was a dreamer.
   He told his wife, "I
have received some
very upsetting
news from
God. There's
going to be a flood all over the world!"
   Noah's wife asked, "Are you sure you
didn't dream this, husband?"
   "No," answered Noah. "I have faith that
this news is from God."

Noah was a tinkerer.

He told his wife, "God has instructed me to build a big ark to save our family from the flood. An ark three stories high made out of gopher wood."

Noah's wife shook her head. "That's a lot of gopher wood to tinker with."

"I know," said Noah. "But I will follow God's instructions and hammer and saw from dawn to dusk."

Noah was a collector.

He told his wife, "God wants me to gather two of every kind of animal, male and female, to ride in the ark with us."

Noah's wife crinkled her nose. "Does that mean collecting slithery snakes and scaly lizards too?"

Noah nodded. "Have courage, dear wife. This is God's will."

A long time passed.

Noah prepared for the flood, and Noah's wife tried to be courageous.

She also tried to help her husband by caring for the animals he was gathering.

That was quite a job because there were so many of them.

She fed them, petted them, sang to them, and put them to bed each night.

But sometimes she
would get exasperated with Noah.
    When their oldest son celebrated his
eighth birthday, Noah missed the party.

He got lost in the jungle looking for leopards to take in the ark.

Then there was the time Noah left the gate unlocked and the female elephant escaped.

She ran through the vegetable garden and mashed all of the prize cucumbers Noah's wife had so patiently tended.

After God told Noah to build the ark, things were never again peaceful around the house.

The sound of hammering and sawing went on constantly. And there were big piles of gopher wood everywhere.

As the ark got larger, Noah and his wife got older. Their sons grew up and found wives of their own.

But one thing never changed.

When Noah's wife went to market, the townspeople would always laugh and point.

"There's Noah's wife. She's married to that crazy man who's building a boat that's too big to fish in and who has thousands of loud, messy animals running all over his property. Who says we're all going to get wet."

When she heard talk like this, Noah's wife would get exasperated.

"My husband is kind and courageous," she would say. "He is following God's command. You are the ones of little faith."

Once one of the townspeople threw a rotten apple at Noah's wife.

She brushed the sticky fruit off her robe and walked home with her head held high.

Another time she heard a group of women laughing as she passed by.

This time she held her head even higher.

Finally, the ark was built, and all the animals were collected. There were no more sounds of pounding and hammering. The piles of gopher wood were gone.

One day when Noah's wife was picking cucumbers from her garden, it began to rain.

As it had never rained before.

The water came down from the sky in silver sheets.

"Look!" said Noah. "It is just as God said."

So Noah and his wife and their sons and their wives boarded the ark. They brought with them the animals Noah had collected, even the slithery snakes and the scaly lizards.

And they brought food and supplies to last for a very long time.

Because not even Noah knew how long the flood would last.

The rains fell for forty days and forty nights. Gray, angry water filled the deepest valley and covered the tallest mountain.

The ark kept Noah and his family and all the animals safe and dry. Noah had built it well, according to God's instructions.

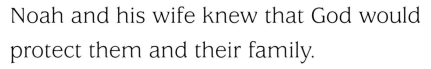

Noah and his wife knew that God would protect them and their family.

But it was a frightening time, and they were glad to have one another to hug.

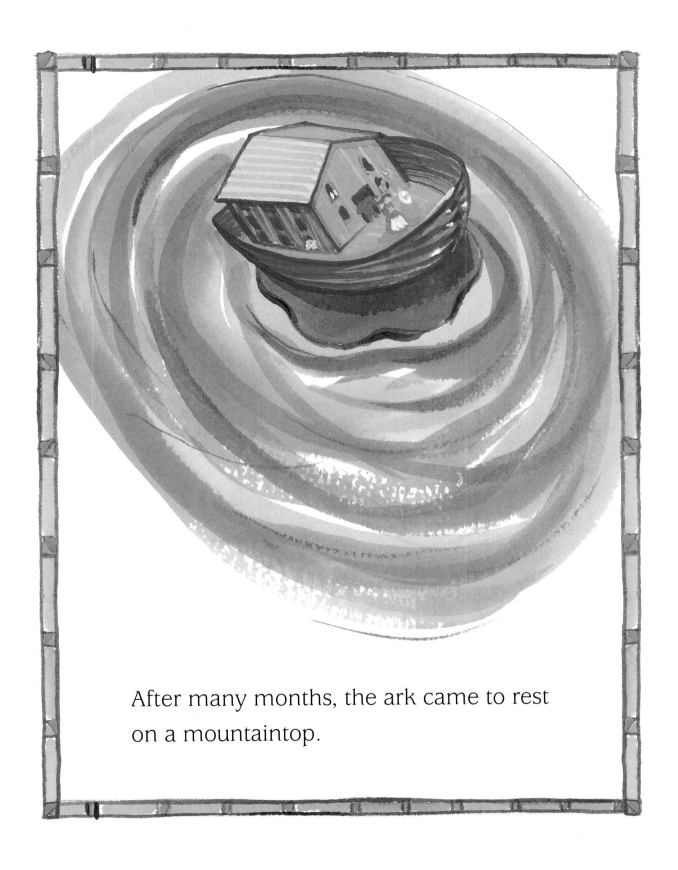

After many months, the ark came to rest
on a mountaintop.

After a few more months, when the tops of the mountains could be seen, Noah said, "I will send this strong black raven to find dry land." (Noah liked ravens.)

Noah's wife got exasperated. "The raven isn't the bird for the job." (She especially liked the gentle, dependable dove.)

Noah sent the raven anyway. That didn't work out.

Then he sent the dove. That didn't work, either.

Noah's wife sighed.

She certainly knew about waiting from all her years of living with Noah.

"It's just not time," she said. "Wait a few days, and then send the dove out again, dear husband."

Noah took his wife's advice.

Seven days later he sent the dove out again, and it came back with an olive leaf in its beak.

The dove had found dry land!

After another seven days, Noah sent out the dove one more time.

But this time it didn't
come back. That meant it
had made a home on the new land.

This was a sign that Noah and his family could leave the ark.

When Noah and his family had herded all the animals off the ark — even the slithery snakes and the scaly lizards — Noah built an altar to God.

Noah's wife
took care of the animals, trying to make
them comfortable in their new home.

*F*inally, Noah's wife rested under a shady tree.

She admired her new surroundings. "Well, dear husband, you weren't dreaming."

She regarded the ark. "And your tinkering was not wasted."

"I love you, dear wife," Noah said, and hugged her tight.

He knew that she had helped him beyond measure.

Then Noah's wife looked up.

God had arched his promise across the
sky. Never again would he send such a
fierce flood. A new world of hope and
love was beginning.

Noah's wife's mouth curved into a
sweet smile as she thought of all the
juicy cucumbers she would grow.